EASY
FRENCH
PHRASE BOOK
Over 750 Basic Phrases
for Everyday Use

DOVER PUBLICATIONS, INC.

NEW YORK

Bibliographical Note

The material in this book was originally published by Dover in 1956 as part of a manual to accompany a recording entitled *Listen & Learn French*. The English outline was prepared by the editorial staff of Dover Publications, Inc. The French translation and transliteration were prepared by Leon J. Cohen.

Library of Congress Cataloging-in-Publication Data

Easy French phrase book : over 750 basic phrases for everyday use.
     p.   cm.
  "Originally published by Dover in 1956 as part of a manual to accompany a recording entitled Listen & learn French. The English outline was prepared by the editorial staff of Dover Publications, Inc. The French translation and transliteration were prepared by Leon J. Cohen"—T.p. verso.
  ISBN-13: 978-0-486-28083-7
  ISBN-10: 0-486-28083-7
  1. French language—Conversation and phrase books—English. I. Dover Publications, Inc.
PC2121.E25 1994
448.3'421—dc20

94-12189
CIP

Manufactured in the United States by Courier Corporation
28083708
www.doverpublications.com

CONTENTS

	PAGE
Introduction	5
French Pronunciation	6
Scheme of Pronunciation	7

	PAGE
Greetings, Introductions and Social Conversation	10
Making Yourself Understood	12
Useful Words and Expressions	13
Difficulties	16
Customs and Baggage	17
Travel: General Expressions	19
Tickets	21
Boat	22
Airplane	23
Taxi	23
Train	24
Bus, Streetcar and Subway	25
Automobile Travel	25
At the Hotel	27
At the Café	31

	PAGE
At the Restaurant	32
Menu	34
Breakfast Foods	35
Soups and Entrées	36
Vegetables and Salad	37
Fruits	38
Beverages	38
Desserts	39
Church	39
Sightseeing	40
Amusements	41
Sports	42
Bank and Money	42
Useful Shopping Information	43
Measurements	46
Colors	46
Stores	47
Bookstore and Stationer's	48
Cigar Store	49
Photography	49
Drugstore	50
Laundry and Dry Cleaning	52
Barber Shop and Beauty Parlor	52
Health and Illness	53
Dentist	54
Post Office	54
Telephone	55
Time and Time Expressions	55
Days of the Week	56
Months and Seasons	56
Numbers	57
Index	59

INTRODUCTION

This book is designed to teach you the basic words, phrases and sentences that you will need for simple everyday communication in France and other French-speaking countries. It does not attempt to teach you the grammatical structure of French, but instead helps you to express your needs and handle problems encountered while traveling.

The value of the book rests as much on what is omitted as on what is included. An effort has been made to include only those phrases pertinent to the needs of the traveler. You will find the phrase "May I have some change" (a frequent need in travel), but do not expect to find a sentence like "This is the pen of my aunt." Furthermore, since the material presented here is not cumulative, as it is in conventional foreign-language courses, you need not start at the beginning. Study whichever phrases will be the most useful to you.

The focus of instruction is on what *you* will say. However, the section entitled "Making Yourself Understood," which contains such vital phrases as "Please speak more slowly" and "Repeat it, please," will aid you in understanding others.

This book is complete in itself and is meant to be used for reference and study. Read it at odd moments and try to learn ten or fifteen phrases a day. Also, be sure to take it with you when you go abroad. All that you have learned will be available for reference and review.

The book is designed to help you form additional French sentences from the sentences it provides. You can do this by substituting a new word for a given word in a familiar sentence. In sentences where this is possible, the candidate for substitution appears (often in parentheses) following the main entry. For example, "The bags on your left (right) are mine" provides two sentences: "The bags on your left are mine" and "The bags on your right are mine."

Another especially helpful feature is the extensive topic and word index beginning on page 59. Notice that each entry in the book is numbered and that the index refers to these numbers. This enables you to locate information you need quickly, without having to search the entire page.

FRENCH PRONUNCIATION

This book uses a phonetic transcription as an aid to correct pronunciation. (See "Scheme of Pronunciation," below.) It usually appears below the French line in the text.

Nasalization

In French, a vowel is nasalized when it is followed by a single *m* or *n* in the same syllable. In our transcription nasalized vowels are rendered:

an, am, em, en	a͞hn
in, im	e͞n
on, om	a͞wn
um, un	u͞hn

Nasalized vowels are made with the breath passing through both the nose and the mouth. You may find that breaking off the vowel suddenly will make the nasalization easier to imitate. Notice that the *m* or *n* is not pronounced after a nasalized vowel.

Silent Final Consonants

In French, a consonant is usually silent at the end of a word. The major exceptions are *c*, *r*, *f* and *l*, which are usually pronounced at the end of a word. (*r* is silent, however, in the endings -*er* and *ier*.)

Liaison

A usually silent final consonant is often pronounced when the following word begins with a vowel or *h*. In such cases, the final consonant is linked to the beginning of the second word. For example, the *s* in *des* is ordinarily silent, but *des olives* is pronounced *day zaw-leev*.

The rules for liaison are complex and the usage is not regular. Study the phonetic transcriptions to get an idea of the word groups that are habitually joined in this manner.

Stress

A French word is most often stressed on the last syllable. However, when the vowel of the last syllable is unstressed *e* (*uh* in our transcription), the word is usually stressed on the next-to-last syllable. In addition to stress within a word, the final syllable of a phrase is given added stress.

SCHEME OF PRONUNCIATION

Letters	Tran- scription	Example	Notes
a	a	as in *a*sk, but cut short	
	ah	as in f*a*ther	
ai	e OR eh	as in m*e*t	
au	oh	as in n*o*tify	See note on *o* below.
b	b	as in *b*oy	
c	k	as in s*k*in	Pronounced *k* before *a, o* or *u*. Do not make a puff of air after the *k* as we do in English.
	s	as in *s*it	Pronounced *s* before *e* and *i*.
ç	s	as in *s*it	
d	d	as in *d*ay	Formed by touching the tongue tip to the teeth, not to the gum ridge behind the teeth as we do in English.
e, è, ê	e OR eh	as in m*e*t	
é	ay	as in d*ay*, but cut short	Pronounce *ay* as a single pure sound, not a diphthong; do not slide over into an *ee* sound as we do in English.

Letters	Tran-scription	Example	Notes
e, eu, œu	uh	as in German *können* (short) or *Goethe* (long)	No exact equivalent in English. Round the lips to say *oh*, and without changing the position of the lips say *eh*.
f	f	as in *f*ather	
g	g, gh	as in *g*o	Before *a, o* and *u*.
	zh	as in a*z*ure	Before *e* and *i*.
gn	ny	as in ca*ny*on	Pronounced as a single sound.
h	—	—	Always silent in French.
i	ee	as in m*ee*t	Pronounce *ee* as a single pure sound, not a diphthong; do not slide over into a *y* sound as we do in English.
j	zh	as in a*z*ure	
k	k	as in s*k*in	Do not make a puff of air after the *k* as we do in English.
l	l	as in *l*et	
m	m	as in *m*et	
n	n	as in *n*ote	
o	aw	as in l*aw*, but cut short	
	oh	as in n*o*tify	Pronounce *oh* as a single pure vowel, not a diphthong; do not slide over into an *oo* sound as we do in English.
oi	wa	as in *wa*nt	
ou	oo	as in f*oo*d	
p	p	as in s*p*in	Do not make a puff of air after the *p* as we do in English.
ph	f	as in *f*ather	

Letters	Tran-scription	Example	Notes
q	k	as in s*k*in	See note on *k* above.
r	r	as in *r*ed	May be rolled with the tip of the tongue as in Italian or Spanish. The Parisian *r*, which resembles the sound of gargling, is produced by vibration of the uvula (the fleshy lobe that hangs in the back of the mouth).
s	s OR ss	as in *s*it	Pronounced *s* at the beginning of a word and when doubled.
	z	as in *z*eal	Pronounced z between vowels.
t	t	as in s*t*ing	Formed by touching the tongue tip to the teeth, not to the gum ridge behind the teeth. Do not make a puff of air after the *t* as we do in English.
th	t	as in s*t*ing	See note on *t* above. Never pronounced like the *th* in English *th*is or *th*in.
u	ew	as in German *ü*ber	No exact equivalent in English. Round the lips to say *oo*, and without changing the position of the lips say *ee*.
v	v	as in *v*ase	
w	v	as in *v*ase	
	w	as in *w*ent	
x	ks	as in pic*ks*	
y	ee	as in m*ee*t	See note on *i* above.
z	z	as in *z*eal	

GREETINGS, INTRODUCTIONS AND SOCIAL CONVERSATION

1. Good morning.
Bonjour.
bawn-zhoor.

2. Good evening.
Bonsoir.
bawn-swahr.

3. Hello.
Bonjour.
bawn-zhoor.

4. Goodbye.
Au revoir.
awr-vwahr.

5. I'll be seeing you.
À bientôt.
ah byen-toh.

6. My name is Charles.
Je m'appelle Charles.
zhuh ma-pel shahrl.

7. I wish to make an appointment with Mr. Desportes.
Je désire prendre rendez-vous avec Monsieur Desportes.
zhuh day-zeer PRAHN-druh rahn-day-voo a-vek muh-syuh day-pawrt.

8. May I introduce Mr. (Mrs., Miss) Simon?
Puis-je vous présenter Monsieur (Madame, Mademoiselle) Simon?
PWEE-zhuh voo pray-zahn-tay muh-syuh (ma-dahm, mad-mwah-zel) see-mawn?

9. —— My wife.
Ma femme.
ma fahm.

10. —— My husband.
Mon mari.
mawn ma-ree.

11. —— My daughter.
Ma fille.
ma FEE-uh.

12. —— My son.
Mon fils.
mawn feess.

13. —— My friend.
Mon ami.
maw na-mee.

14. —— My sister.
Ma sœur.
ma suhr.

15. —— My brother.
Mon frère.
mawn frehr.

16. —— My child.
Mon enfant.
maw nahn-fahn.

17. The boy.
Le garçon.
luh gar-sawn.

18. The girl.
La jeune fille.
la zhuhn FEE-yuh.

19. The man.
L'homme.
lawm.

20. The woman.
La femme.
la fahm.

21. I am glad to know you.
Je suis heureux de faire votre connaissance.
zhuh swee zuh-ruh duh fehr VAW-truh kawn-nes-sahnss.

22. I am here on a business trip.
Je suis ici en voyage d'affaires.
zhuh swee zee-see ahn vwah-yazh da-fehr.

23. —— On a vacation.
En vacances.
ahn va-kahnss.

24. We are traveling to Rouen.
Nous allons à Rouen.
noo zal-lawn zah roo-ahn.

25. I am a friend of Robert's.
Je suis un ami de Robert.
zhuh swee zuh na-mee duh raw-behr.

26. How are you?
Comment allez-vous?
kaw-mahn tal-lay-voo?

27. Fine, thanks.   And you?
Très bien, merci.   Et vous?
treh byen, mehr-see.   ay voo?

28. How are things?
Comment ça va?
kaw-mahn sa va?

29. All right.
Ça va.
sa va.

30. So, so.
Comme ci, comme ça.
kawm see, kawm sa.

31. How is your family?
Comment va votre famille?
kaw-mahn va VAW-truh fa-MEE-yuh?

32. Very well.
Très bien.
treh byen.

33. Please sit down.
Veuillez vous asseoir.
vuh-yay voo za-swahr.

34. I have enjoyed myself very much.
J'ai passé un moment très agréable.
zhay pa-say uhn maw-mahn treh za-gray-AH-bluh.

35. Give my regards to your aunt and uncle.
Mes amitiés à votre tante et à votre oncle.
may za-mee-tyay ah VAW-truh tahnt ay ah vaw TRAWN-kluh.

36. Come to see us.
Venez nous voir.
vuh-nay noo vwahr.

37. Give me your address and telephone number.
Donnez-moi votre adresse et votre numéro de
téléphone.
*daw-nay-mwah vaw-tra-dress ay VAW-truh new-may-roh
duh tay-lay-fawn.*

38. May I call on you again?
Puis-je revenir vous voir?
PWEE-zhuh ruh-vuh-neer voo vwahr?

39. I like you very much.
Vous m'êtes très sympathique.
voo met treh sen-pa-teek.

MAKING YOURSELF UNDERSTOOD

40. Do you speak English?
Parlez-vous anglais?
par-lay-voo ahn-gleh?

41. Does anyone here speak English?
Y a-t-il quelqu'un ici qui parle anglais?
ee a-teel kel-kuhn ee-see kee par lahn-gleh?

42. I speak only English.
Je ne parle que l'anglais.
zhuh nuh parl kuh lahn-gleh.

43. I speak a little French.
Je parle un peu français.
zhuh parl uhn puh frahn-seh.

44. Please speak more slowly.
Veuillez parler plus lentement.
vuh-yay par-lay plew lahnt-mahn.

45. I (do not) understand.
Je (ne) comprends (pas).
zhuh (nuh) kawn-prahn (pah).

46. Do you understand me?
Me comprenez-vous?
muh kawn-pruh-nay-voo?

47. Repeat it, please.
Veuillez répéter, s'il vous plaît.
vuh-yay ray-pay-tay, seel voo pleh.

48. Write it down, please.
Écrivez-le, s'il vous plaît.
ay-kree-vay-luh, seel voo pleh.

49. What does this mean?
Que veut dire ceci?
kuh vuh deer suh-see?

50. What is that?
Qu'est-ce que c'est que ça?
kes-kuh seh kuh sa?

51. How do you say "pencil" in French?
Comment dit-on "pencil" en français?
kaw-mahn dee-tawn "pencil" ahn frahn-seh?

52. How do you spell "Chateaubriand"?
Comment épelez-vous "Chateaubriand"?
kaw-mahn tay-play-voo "sha-toh-bree-ahn"?

USEFUL WORDS AND EXPRESSIONS

53. Yes.
Oui.
wee.

54. No.
Non.
nawn.

55. Perhaps.
Peut-être.
puh-TEH-truh.

56. Please.
S'il vous plaît.
seel voo pleh.

57. Excuse me.
Pardon.
par-dawn.

58. Thanks (very much).
Merci (beaucoup).
mehr-see (boh-koo).

59. You are welcome.
De rien.
duh ree-en.

60. I am a United States citizen.
Je suis Américain.
zhuh swee za-may-ree-ken.

61. My (mailing) address is 20 Park Street.
Mon adresse (pour le courrier) est rue du Parc,
   numéro vingt.
*maw na-dress (poor luh koor-yay) eh rew dew park,
   new-may-roh ven.*

62. What do you wish?
Que désirez-vous?
kuh day-zee-ray-voo?

63. Come here.
Venez ici.
vuh-nay zee-see.

64. Come in.
Entrez.
ahn-tray.

65. Wait a moment.
Attendez un moment.
at-tahn-day zuhn maw-mahn.

66. I am in a hurry.
Je suis pressé.
zhuh swee pres-say.

67. I am warm, cold.
J'ai chaud, froid.
zhay shoh, frwah.

68. I am hungry, thirsty.
J'ai faim, soif.
zhay fen, swahf.

69. I am busy, tired.
Je suis occupé, fatigué.
zhuh swee zaw-kew-pay, fa-tee-gay.

70. I am glad.
J'en suis content.
zhahn swee kawn-tahn.

71. I am sorry.
Je regrette.
zhuh ruh-gret.

72. What is the matter here?
Qu'y a-t-il?
kee a-teel?

73. It is all right.
C'est bien.
seh byen.

74. I (do not) know.
Je (ne) sais (pas).
zhuh (nuh) say (pah).

75. I (do not) think so.
Je (ne) le crois (pas).
zhuh (nuh) luh krwah (pah).

76. It doesn't matter.
Ça ne fait rien.
sa nuh feh ree-en.

77. How much is it?
Combien est-ce?
kawn-byen ess?

78. That is all.
C'est tout.
seh too.

79. Can you help me (tell me)?
Pouvez-vous m'aider (me dire)?
poo-vay-voo may-day (muh deer)?

80. Where is the washroom?
Où sont les lavabos?
oo sawn lay la-va-boh?

81. The men's room.
Messieurs.
may-syuh.

82. The ladies' room.
Dames.
dahm.

83. I am looking for my hotel.
Je cherche mon hôtel.
zhuh shehrsh maw no-tel.

84. I should like to walk there.
Je voudrais y aller à pied.
zhuh voo-dreh zee al-lay ah pyay.

85. Why?
Pourquoi?
poor-kwah?

86. When?
Quand?
kahn?

87. Who?
Qui?
kee?

88. What?
Quoi?
kwah?

89. How?
Comment?
kaw-mahn?

90. How long?
Combien de temps?
kawn-byen duh tahn?

91. How far?
À quelle distance?
ah kel deess-tahns?

92. Here.
Ici.
ee-see.

93. There.
Là.
la.

94. To.
À.
ah.

95. From.
De.
duh.

96. With.
Avec.
a-vek.

97. Without.
Sans.
sahn.

98. In.
Dans.
dahn.

99. On.
Sur.
sewr.

100. Near.
Près de.
preh duh.

101. Far.
Loin de.
lwen duh.

102. In front of.
Devant.
duh-vahn.

103. Behind.
Derrière.
deh-ryehr.

104. Beside.
À côté de.
ah koh-tay duh.

105. Inside.
À l'intérieur.
ah len-tay-ryuhr.

106. Outside.
À l'extérieur.
ah lex-tay-ryuhr.

107. Empty.
Vide.
veed.

108. Full.
Plein.
plen.

109. Something.
Quelque chose.
kel-kuh shohz.

110. Nothing.
Rien.
ree-en.

111. Several.
Plusieurs.
plew-zyuhr.

112. Few.
Quelques.
kel-kuh.

113. (Much) more.
(Beaucoup) plus.
(boh-koo) plewss.

114. Less.
Moins.
mwen.

115. (A little) more.
(Un peu) plus.
(uhn puh) plewss.

116. Enough.
Assez.
as-say.

117. Too much.
Trop.
troh.

118. Many.
Beaucoup.
boh-koo.

119. Good.
Bon.
bawn.

120. Better (than).
Meilleur (que).
may-yuhr (kuh).

121. Best.
Le meilleur.
luh may-yuhr.

122. Bad.
Mauvais.
moh-veh.

123. Worse (than).
Pire (que).
peer (kuh).

124. Now.
Maintenant.
ment-nahn.

125. Immediately.
Tout de suite.
toot sweet.

126. Soon.
Bientôt.
byen-toh.

127. Later.
Plus tard.
plew tahr.

128. As soon as possible.
Le plus tôt possible.
luh plew toh paw-SEE-bluh.

129. It is (too) late.
Il est (trop) tard.
eel eh (troh) tahr.

130. It is early.
Il est tôt.
eel eh toh.

131. Slowly.
Lentement.
lahnt-mahn.

132. Slower.
Plus lentement.
plew lahnt-mahn.

133. Quickly.
Vite.
veet.

134. Faster.
Plus vite.
plew veet.

135. Look out!
Attention!
ah-tahn-syawn.

136. Listen.
Écoutez.
ay-koo-tay.

137. Look here.
Regardez.
ruh-gar-day.

DIFFICULTIES

138. I cannot find my hotel address.
Je ne peux pas trouver l'adresse de mon hôtel.
zhuh nuh puh pah troo-vay la-dress duh maw no-tel.

139. I have lost my friends.
J'ai perdu mes amis.
zhay pehr-dew may za-mee.

140. **I left my purse, wallet in the hotel.**
J'ai laissé mon sac, mon portefeuille à l'hôtel.
zhay les-say mawn sahk, mawn pawrt-FUH-yuh ah lo-tel.

141. **I forgot my money, keys.**
J'ai oublié mon argent, mes clés.
zhay oo-blee-ay maw nar-zhahn, may klay.

142. **I have missed my train.**
J'ai manqué mon train.
zhay mahn-kay mawn tren.

143. **What am I to do?**
Que dois-je faire?
kuh DWAH-zhuh fehr?

144. **My glasses are broken.**
Mes lunettes sont cassées.
may lew-net sawn kas-say.

145. **Where can they be repaired?**
Où peut-on les faire réparer?
oo puh-tawn lay fehr ray-pa-ray?

146. **A hearing aid.**
Un appareil acoustique.
uh nap-pa-ray a-kooss-teek.

147. **The lost-and-found desk.**
Le bureau des objets trouvés.
luh bew-roh day zawb-zheh troo-vay.

148. **The American consulate.**
Le consulat des États-Unis.
luh kawn-sew-la day zay-ta-zew-nee.

149. **The police station.**
Le commissariat de police.
luh kaw-mee-sa-rya duh paw-leess.

150. **I will call a policeman.**
Je vais appeler un agent.
zhuh vay za-play uh na-zhahn.

CUSTOMS AND BAGGAGE

151. **Where is the customs?**
Où est la douane?
oo eh la doo-an?

152. **Here is my baggage, five pieces.**
Voici mes bagages, cinq pièces.
vwah-see may ba-gazh, sen pyess.

153. —— **My passport.**
Mon passeport.
mawn pass-pawr.

154. —— **My identification papers.**
Mes papiers d'identité.
may pa-pyay dee-dahn-tee-tay.

155. —— **My health certificate.**
Mon certificat de santé.
mawn sehr-tee-fee-ka duh sahn-tay.

156. The bags on your left (right) are mine.
Les valises à votre gauche (droite) m'appartiennent.
lay va-leez zah VAW-truh gohsh (drwaht) ma-par-tyen.

157. I have nothing to declare.
Je n'ai rien à déclarer.
zhuh nay ree-eh nah day-kla-ray.

158. All this is for my personal use.
Tout ceci est pour mon usage personnel.
too suh-see eh poor maw new-zazh pehr-saw-nel.

159. Must I open everything?
Dois-je tout ouvrir?
DWAH-zhuh too too-vreer?

160. I cannot open that.
Je ne peux pas l'ouvrir.
zhuh nuh puh pas loo-vreer.

161. There is nothing here but clothing.
Il n'y a rien ici que des vêtements.
eel nee a ree-en ee-see kuh day vet-mahn.

162. These are gifts.
Ce sont des cadeaux.
suh sawn day ka-doh.

163. Are these things dutiable?
Ces objets sont-ils passibles de droits de douane?
say zawb-zheh sawn-teel pa-SEE-bluh duh drwah duh doo-an?

164. How much must I pay?
Combien dois-je payer?
kawn-byen DWAH-zhuh peh-yay?

165. This is all I have.
C'est tout ce que j'ai.
seh too skuh zhay.

166. Have you finished?
Avez-vous fini?
a-vay-voo fee-nee?

167. I cannot find my baggage.
Je ne peux pas trouver mes bagages.
zhuh nuh puh pah troo-vay may ba-gazh.

168. Where is the baggage checked to destination?
Où enregistre-t-on les bagages?
oo ahn-ruh-ZHEE-struh-tawn lay ba-gazh?

169. The baggage room.
La salle des bagages.
la sal day ba-gazh.

170. The check room.
La consigne.
la kawn-SEEN-yuh.

171. The baggage check.
Le billet des bagages.
luh bee-yeh day ba-gazh.

172. I want to leave these bags for a while.
Je désire laisser ces valises en consigne.
zhuh day-zeer les-say say va-leez ahn kawn-SEEN-yuh.

TRAVEL:
GENERAL EXPRESSIONS

173. I want to go to the airline office.
Je désire aller au bureau de la compagnie d'aviation.
zhuh day-zee ral-lay oh bew-roh duh la kawn-pan-yee da-vee-ah-syawn.

174. —— The airport.
L'aérodrome.
la-ay-raw-drohm.

175. —— The bus station.
La gare des autobus.
la gar day zaw-toh-bewss.

176. —— The dock.
Le quai.
luh kay.

177. —— The railroad station.
La gare.
la gar.

178. How long does it take to go to Chartres?
Combien de temps faut-il pour aller à Chartres?
kawn-byen duh tahn foh-teel poor al-lay ah SHAR-truh?

179. When will we arrive at Cherbourg?
Quand arriverons-nous à Cherbourg?
kahn ah-ree-vuh-rawn-noo ah shehr-boor?

180. Is this the direct way to Versailles?
Est-ce la route directe de Versailles?
ess la root dee-rekt duh vehr-SAH-yuh?

181. Please show me the way to the business section.
Pouvez-vous m'indiquer le chemin du quartier des affaires,
s'il vous plaît?
*poo-vay-voo men-dee-kay luh shuh-men dew kar-tyay day za-fehr,
seel voo pleh?*

182. —— To the residential section.
Du quartier résidentiel.
dew kar-tyay ray-zee-dahn-syel.

183. —— To the shopping section.
Du quartier des magasins.
dew kar-tyay day ma-ga-zen.

184. —— To the city.
De la ville.
duh la veel.

185. —— To the village.
Du village.
dew veel-lazh.

186. Where do I turn?
Où dois-je tourner?
oo DWAH-zhuh toor-nay?

187. —— To the north.
Au nord.
oh nawr.

188. —— To the south.
Au sud.
oh sewd.

189. —— To the west.
À l'ouest.
ah lwest.

190. —— To the east.
À l'est.
ah lest.

191. —— To the right.
À droite.
ah drwaht.

192. —— To the left.
À gauche.
ah gohsh.

193. —— At the traffic light.
À la lumière.
ah la lewm-yehr.

194. Where is it?
Où est-ce?
oo ess?

195. Is it on this side of the street?
Est-ce de ce côté-ci de la rue?
ess duh suh koh-tay-see duh la rew?

196. —— On the other side of the street?
De l'autre côté de la rue?
duh LOH-truh koh-tay duh la rew?

197. —— Across the street?
En face?
en fass?

198. —— At the corner?
Au coin de la rue?
oh kwen duh la rew?

199. —— In the middle?
Au milieu?
oh meel-yuh?

200. —— Straight ahead.
Tout droit.
too drwah.

201. —— Forward.
En avant.
ah na-vahn.

202. —— Back.
En arrière.
ah na-ree-ehr.

203. Am I going in the right direction?
Est-ce la bonne direction?
ess la bawn dee-rek-syawn?

204. What street is this?
Quelle est cette rue?
keh leh set rew?

205. The circle.
Le rond-point.
luh rawn-pwen.

206. The place.
La place.
la plass.

207. The avenue.
L'avenue.
la-vuh-new.

TICKETS

208. Where is the ticket office?
Où est le guichet?
oo eh luh ghee-sheh?

209. How much is a ticket to Marseilles?
Combien coûte un billet pour Marseille?
kawn-byen koot uhn bee-yeh poor mar-SAY-yuh?

210. One-way ticket.
Un billet d'aller.
uhn bee-yeh dal-lay.

211. Round trip.
D'aller et retour.
dal-lay ay ruh-toor.

212. First class.
Première classe.
pruh-myehr klass.

213. Second class.
Seconde classe.
suh-gawnd klass.

214. Third class.
Troisième classe.
trwah-zyem klass.

215. Local.
L'omnibus.
lawm-nee-bews.

216. Express.
Le rapide.
luh ra-peed.

217. A reserved seat.
Une place réservée.
ewn plass ray-zehr-vay.

218. Can I go by way of Lyons?
Puis-je y aller en passant par Lyon?
pwee-zhee al-lay ahn pa-sahn par lee-awn?

219. May I stop on the way?
Puis-je m'arrêter en route?
PWEE-zhuh ma-reh-tay ahn root?

BOAT

220. Can I go by boat to London?
Puis-je aller à Londres par bateau?
pwee-zha-lay ah LAWN-druh par ba-toh?

221. When does the next boat leave?
Quand part le prochain bateau?
kahn par luh praw-shen ba-toh?

222. When must I go on board?
À quelle heure dois-je m'embarquer?
ah keh luhr DWAH-zhuh mahn-bar-kay?

223. Can I land at le Havre?
Pourrai-je débarquer au Havre?
poor-RAY-zhuh day-bar-kay oh AH-vruh?

224. The captain.
Le capitaine.
luh ka-pee-ten.

225. The purser.
Le commissaire.
luh kaw-mee-sehr.

226. The steward.
Le garçon.
luh gar-sawn.

227. The deck.
Le pont.
luh pawn.

228. The cabin.
La cabine.
la ka-been.

229. The lifeboat.
Le canot de sauvetage.
luh ka-noh duh sohv-tazh.

230. The life preserver.
La ceinture de sauvetage.
la sen-tewr duh sohv-tazh.

231. I am seasick.
J'ai le mal de mer.
zhay luh mal duh mehr.

AIRPLANE

232. Is there a bus service to the airport?
Y a-t-il un service d'autobus pour l'aéroport?
ee a-tee luhn sehr-veess daw-toh-bewss poor la-ay-raw- pawr?

233. At what time will they come for me?
À quelle heure viendra-t-on me chercher?
ah keh luhr vyen-dra-tawn muh shehr-shay?

234. When is there a plane to Rome?
À quelle heure y a-t-il un départ pour Rome?
ah keh luhr ee a-teel uhn day-par poor rawm?

235. Is food served on the plane?
Peut-on obtenir de quoi manger à bord?
puh-taw nawp-tuh-neer duh kwah mahn-zhay ah bawr?

236. How many kilos may I take?
Combien de kilos de bagages puis-je emporter?
kawn-byen duh kee-loh duh ba-gazh PWEE-zhuh ahn-pawr-tay?

237. How much per kilogram for excess?
Combien par kilo pour l'excédent?
kawn-byen par kee-loh poor lek-say-dahn?

TAXI

238. Please call a taxi for me.
Veuillez m'appeler un taxi.
vuh-yay map-lay uhn tak-see.

239. How far is it?
À quelle distance est-ce?
ah kel dees-tahnss ess?

240. How much will it cost?
Quel sera le prix?
kel suh-ra luh pree?

241. What do you charge per hour (kilometer)?
Combien prenez-vous de l'heure (du kilomètre)?
kawn-byen pruh-nay-voo duh luhr (dew kee-law-MEH- truh)?

242. Please drive more slowly (carefully).
Veuillez conduire plus lentement (prudemment).
vuh-yay kawn-dweer plew lahnt-mahn (prew-da-mahn).

243. Stop here.
Arrêtez ici.
ar-reh-tay zee-see.

244. Wait for me.
Attendez-moi.
at-tahn-day-mwah.

TRAIN

245. Where is the railroad station?
Où est la gare?
oo eh la gar?

246. When does the train for Lyons leave?
À quelle heure part le train pour Lyon?
ah keh luhr par luh tren poor lee-awn?

247. The boat train.
Le train-paquebot.
luh tren-pak-boh.

248. Where does the train leave?
D'où part le train?
doo par luh tren?

249. Please open the window.
Voulez-vous bien ouvrir la fenêtre?
voo-lay-voo byen oo-vreer la fuh-NEH-truh?

250. Close the window.
Fermez la fenêtre.
fehr-may la fuh-NEH-truh.

251. Where is the diner?
Où est le wagon-restaurant?
oo eh luh va-gawn-ress-taw-rahn?

252. May I smoke?
Puis-je fumer?
PWEE-zhuh few-may?

BUS, STREETCAR AND SUBWAY

253. What bus do I take to Montmartre?
Quel autobus dois-je prendre pour aller à Montmartre?
*keh law-toh-bewss DWAH-zhuh PRAHN-druh poor
al-lay ah mawn-MAR-truh?*

254. The bus stop.
L'arrêt d'autobus.
lar-reh daw-toh-bewss.

255. The driver.
Le conducteur.
luh kawn-dewk-tuhr.

256. A transfer.
Une correspondance.
ewn kaw-ress-pawn-dahns.

257. Where does the subway for l'Étoile stop?
Où s'arrête le métro pour l'Étoile?
oo sar-ret luh may-troh poor lay-twahl?

258. Do you go near the Champs Elysées?
Passez-vous près des Champs-Elysées?
pas-say-voo preh day shahn-zay-lee-zay?

259. Do I have to change?
Dois-je changer?
DWAH-zhuh shahn-zhay?

260. Please tell me where to get off.
Veuillez me dire où il faut descendre.
vuh-yay muh deer oo eel foh day-SAHN-druh.

261. Off next stop, please.
Le prochain arrêt, s'il vous plaît.
luh praw-shen ar-reh, seel voo pleh.

AUTOMOBILE TRAVEL

262. Where can we rent a car?
Où pouvons-nous louer une automobile?
oo poo-vawn-noo loo-ay ew naw-toh-maw-beel?

263. I have an international driver's license.
J'ai un permis international.
zhay uhn pehr-mee en-tehr-na-syaw-nal.

264. Can you recommend a good mechanic?
Pouvez-vous m'indiquer un bon mécanicien?
poo-vay-voo men-dee-kay uhn bawn may-ka-nee-syen?

265. —— A gas station.
Un poste d'essence.
uhn pawst des-sahnss.

266. —— A garage.
Un garage.
uhn ga-razh.

267. Is the road good?
La route est-elle bonne?
la root eh-tel bawn?

268. Where does that road go?
Où va cette route?
oo va set root?

269. What town is this?
Comment s'appelle cette ville?
kawn-mahn sa-pel set veel?

270. The next one?
La prochaine?
la praw-shen?

271. Can you draw me a map?
Pouvez-vous me dessiner un plan?
poo-vay-voo muh des-see-nay uhn plahn?

272. How much is gas a liter?
Combien le litre d'essence?
kawn-byen luh LEE-truh des-sahnss?

273. Give me ten liters.
Donnez-moi dix litres.
daw-nay-mwah dee LEE-truh.

274. Please change the oil.
Veuillez changer l'huile.
vuh-yay shahn-zhay lweel.

275. Put water in the battery.
Mettez de l'eau dans les accus.
met-tay duh loh dahn lay za-kew.

276. Will you lubricate the car?
Voulez-vous bien graisser la voiture?
voo-lay-voo byen gres-say la vwah-tewr?

277. Adjust the brakes.
Ajustez les freins.
ah-zhew-stay lay fren.

278. Will you check the tires?
Voulez-vous bien regarder les pne
voo-lay-voo byen ruh-gar-day lay pnuh.

279. Can you fix the flat tire?
Pouvez-vous réparer le pneu crevé?
poo-vay-voo ray-pa-ray luh pnuh kruh-vay?

280. —— A puncture.
Une crevaison.
ewn kruh-vay-zawn.

281. —— A slow leak.
Une légère fuite.
ewn lay-zhehr fweet.

282. The engine overheats.
Le moteur chauffe.
luh maw-tuhr shohf.

283. The engine misses (stalls).
Le moteur rate (cale).
luh maw-tuhr raht (kal).

284. May I park here for a while?
Puis-je stationner ici un instant?
PWEE-zhuh sta-syaw-nay ee-see uh nen-stahn?

AT THE HOTEL

285. I am looking for a good hotel.
Je cherche un bon hôtel.
zhuh shehrsh uhn baw noh-tel.

286. —— An inexpensive hotel.
Un hôtel à prix modérés.
uh noh-tel ah pree maw-day-ray.

287. —— A boarding house.
Une pension.
ewn pahn-syawn.

288. —— A furnished apartment.
Un appartement meublé.
uh nap-par-tuh-mahn muh-blay.

289. I (do not) want to be at the center of town.
Je (ne) veux (pas) être au centre de la ville.
zhuh (nuh) vuh (pah) ZEH-truh oh SAHN-truh duh la veel.

290. Where it is not noisy.
Où il n'y a pas de bruit.
oo eel nee a pah duh brwee.

291. I have a reservation for today.
J'ai réservé une chambre pour aujourd'hui.
zhay ray-zehr-vay ewn SHAHN-bruh poor oh-zhoord-wee.

292. Do you have a room, a vacancy?
Avez-vous une chambre, une vacance?
a-vay-voo zewn SHAHN-bruh, ewn va-kahnss?

293. —— An air-conditioned room.
Une chambre climatisée.
ewn SHAHN-bruh klee-ma-tee-zay.

294. —— A single room.
Une chambre à un lit.
ewn SHAHN-brah uhn lee.

295. —— A double room.
Une chambre pour deux personnes.
ewn SHAHN-bruh poor duh pehr-sawn.

296. —— With meals.
Avec repas.
a-vek ruh-pah.

297. —— Without meals.
Sans repas.
sahn ruh-pah.

298. —— With a double bed.
À un grand lit.
ah uhn grahn lee.

299. —— With bath.
Avec salle de bain.
a-vek sal duh ben.

300. —— With a shower.
Avec une douche.
a-vek ewn doosh.

301. —— With twin beds.
Avec lits jumeaux.
a-vek lee zhew-moh.

302. —— A suite.
Un appartement.
uh nap-par-tuh-mahn.

303. —— For tonight.
Pour cette nuit.
poor set nwee.

304. —— For three days.
Pour trois jours.
poor trwah zhoor.

305. —— For two persons.
Pour deux personnes.
poor duh pehr-sawn.

306. What is the rate per day?
Quel est votre prix par jour?
keh leh VAW-truh pree par zhoor?

307. Are tax and room service included?
Est-ce que les taxes et le service sont compris?
ess-kuh lay tax ay luh sehr-veess sawn kawn-pree?

308. I should like to see the room.
Je voudrais bien voir la chambre.
zhuh voo-dreh byen vwahr la SHAHN-bruh.

309. I do not like this one.
Je n'aime pas celle-ci.
zhuh nem pah sel-see.

310. Upstairs.
En haut.
ahn oh.

311. Downstairs.
En bas.
ahn bah.

312. Is there an elevator?
Y a-t-il un ascenseur?
ee a-tee luh na-sahn-suhr?

313. Will you send for my bags?
Voulez-vous bien envoyer chercher mes bagages?
voo-lay-voo byen ahn-vwah-yay shehr-shay may ba-gazh?

314. Room service, please.
Le service, s'il vous plaît.
luh sehr-veess, seel voo pleh.

315. Please send a porter to my room.
Faites monter un porteur dans ma chambre, s'il vous plaît.
fet mawn-tay uhn pawr-tuhr dahn ma SHAHN-bruh, seel voo pleh.

316. —— A chambermaid.
Une femme de chambre.
ewn fahm duh SHAHN-bruh.

317. —— A bellhop.
Un chasseur.
uhn shas-suhr.

318. Please call me at nine o'clock.
Veuillez m'appeler à neuf heures.
vuh-yay map-lay ah nuh vuhr.

319. I want breakfast in my room.
Je désire avoir le petit déjeuner dans ma chambre.
zhuh day-zeer a-vwahr luh puh-tee day-zhuh-nay dahn ma SHAHN-bruh.

320. Come back later.
Revenez plus tard.
ruh-vuh-nay plew tar.

321. Bring me another blanket.
Apportez-moi encore une couverture.
ap-pawr-tay-mwah ahn-kawr ewn koo-vehr-tewr.

322. A pillow.
Un oreiller.
uh naw-ray-yay.

323. A pillowcase.
Une taie d'oreiller.
ewn tay daw-ray-yay.

324. Hangers.
Des cintres.
day SEN-truh.

325. Soap.
Le savon.
luh sa-vawn.

326. Towels.
Les serviettes.
lay sehr-vee-et.

327. A bath mat.
Un tapis de bain.
uhn ta-pee duh ben.

328. The bathtub.
La baignoire.
la ben-wahr.

329. The sink.
Le lavabo.
luh la-va-boh.

330. Toilet paper.
Le papier hygiénique.
luh pap-yay ee-zhee-ay-neek.

331. I should like to speak to the manager.
Je voudrais bien parler au gérant.
zhuh voo-dreh byen par-lay oh zhay-rahn.

332. My room key, please.
Ma clé, s'il vous plaît?
ma klay, seel voo pleh.

333. Have I any letters or messages?
Y a-t-il des lettres ou des messages pour moi?
ee a-teel day LEH-truh oo day mes-sazh poor mwah?

334. What is my room number?
Quel est le numéro de ma chambre?
keh leh luh new-may-roh duh ma SHAHN-bruh?

335. I am leaving at ten o'clock.
Je pars à dix heures.
zhuh par ah dee zuhr.

336. Please make out my bill.
Veuillez préparer ma note.
vuh-yay pray-pa-ray ma nawt.

337. Will you accept a check?
Voulez-vous bien accepter un chèque?
voo-lay-voo byen ak-sep-tay uhn shek?

338. Please forward my mail to American Express in Rome.
Veuillez faire suivre mon courrier à l'American Express à Rome.
vuh-yay fehr SWEE-vruh mawn koor-yay ah l'American Express a rawm.

339. May I store baggage here until tomorrow?
Puis-je vous laisser des bagages jusqu'à demain?
PWEE-zhuh voo les-say day ba-gazh zhews-kah duh_men?

AT THE CAFÉ

340. The bartender.
Le barman.
luh bar-mahn.

341. A drink.
Une boisson.
ewn bwah-sawn.

342. A fruit drink.
Un jus de fruit.
uhn zhew duh frwee.

343. A soft drink.
Une boisson gazeuse.
ewn bwah-sawn ga-zuhz.

344. A bottle of mineral water.
Une bouteille d'eau minérale.
ewn boo-tay doh mee-nay-ral.

345. A glass of port.
Un verre de porto.
uhn vehr duh pawr-toh.

346. Some beer (light, dark).
De la bière (blonde, brune).
duh la byehr (blawnd, brewn).

347. Some wine (red, white).
Du vin (rouge, blanc).
dew ven (roozh, blahn).

348. Let's have another.
Prenons-en un autre.
pruh-nawn zahn uh NOH-truh.

349. To your health!
À votre santé!
ah VAW-truh sahn-tay!

AT THE RESTAURANT

350. Where is there a good restaurant?
Où peut-on trouver un bon restaurant?
oo puh-tawn troo-vay uhn bawn ress-taw-rahn?

351. Breakfast.
Le petit déjeuner.
luh puh-tee day-zhuh-nay.

352. Lunch.
Le déjeuner.
luh day-zhuh-nay.

353. Dinner.
Le dîner.
luh dee-nay.

354. Supper.
Le souper.
luh soo-pay.

355. A sandwich.
Un sandwich.
uhn sahnd-weetsh.

356. A snack.
Un casse-croûte.
uhn kass-kroot.

357. At what time is dinner served?
À quelle heure servez-vous le dîner?
ah keh luhr sehr-vay-voo luh dee-nay?

358. Can we lunch (dine) now?
Pouvons-nous déjeuner (dîner) maintenant?
poo-vawn-noo day-zhuh-nay (dee-nay) ment-nahn?

359. The waitress.
La serveuse.
la sehr-vuhz.

360. The waiter.
Le garçon.
luh gar-sawn.

361. The headwaiter.
Le maître d'hôtel.
luh MEH-truh doh-tel.

362. Waiter!
Garçon!
gar-sawn!

363. There are two of us.
Nous sommes deux.
noo sawm duh.

364. Give me a table near the window.
Donnez-moi une table près de la fenêtre.
daw-nay-mwah ewn TA-bluh preh duh la fuh-NEH-truh.

365. We want to dine à la carte.
Nous voulons dîner à la carte.
noo voo-lawn dee-nay ah la kart.

366. —— Table d'hôte.
À prix fixe.
ah pree feeks.

367. Please serve us quickly.
Servez-nous vite, s'il vous plaît.
sehr-vay-noo veet, seel voo pleh.

368. Bring me the menu.
Apportez-moi le menu.
ap-pawr-tay-mwah luh muh-new.

369. —— The wine list.
La carte des vins.
la kart day ven.

370. —— A fork.
Une fourchette.
ewn foor-shet.

371. —— A knife.
Un couteau.
uhn koo-toh.

372. —— A plate.
Une assiette.
ewn as-syet.

373. —— A teaspoon.
Une cuillère à café.
ewn kwee-yeh rah ka-fay.

374. —— A large spoon.
Une cuillère à soupe.
ewn kwee-yeh rah soop.

375. I want something simple.
Je désire quelque chose de simple.
zhuh day-zeer kel-kuh shohz duh SEN-pluh.

376. —— Not too spicy.
Pas trop épicé.
pah troh pay-pee-say.

377. I like the meat rare.
J'aime la viande saignante.
zhem la vee-ahnd sen-yahnt.

378. —— Well done.
Bien cuite.
byen kweet.

379. Take it away, please.
Emportez cela, s'il vous plaît.
ahn-pawr-tay suh-la, seel voo pleh.

380. This is cold.
C'est froid.
seh frwah.

381. I did not order this.
Je n'ai pas commandé cela.
zhuh nay pah kaw-mahn-day suh-la.

382. May I change this for a salad?
Pouvez-vous remplacer cela par une salade?
poo-vay-voo rahn-pla-say suh-la par ewn sa-lad?

383. Ask the headwaiter to come here.
Priez le maître d'hôtel de venir.
pree-ay luh MEH-truh doh-tel duh vuh-neer.

384. The check, please.
L'addition, s'il vous plaît.
la-dee-syawn, seel voo pleh.

385. Is the tip included?
Le pourboire, est-il compris?
luh poor-bwahr, eh-teel kawn-pree?

386. Is the service charge included?
Le service, est-il compris?
luh sehr-veess, eh-teel kawn-pree?

387. There is a mistake in the bill.
Il y a une erreur dans l'addition.
eel ya ewn ehr-ruhr dahn la-dee-syawn.

388. What are these charges for?
Pourquoi ces suppléments?
poor-kwah say sew-play-mahn?

389. Keep the change.
Gardez la monnaie.
gar-day la maw-neh.

390. The food and service were excellent.
La cuisine et le service étaient excellents.
la kwee-zeen ay luh sehr-veess ay-teh tex-eh-lahn.

MENU

391. Drinking water.
L'eau potable.
loh paw-TA-bluh.

392. —— With ice.
Avec de la glace.
a-vek duh la glas.

393. —— Without ice.
Sans glace.
sahn glas.

394. The bread.
Le pain.
luh pen.

395. The butter.
Le beurre.
luh buhr.

396. The sugar.
Le sucre.
luh SEW-kruh.

397. The salt.
Le sel.
luh sel.

398. The pepper.
Le poivre.
luh PWAH-vruh.

399. The sauce.
La sauce.
la sohss.

400. The oil.
L'huile.
lweel.

401. The vinegar.
Le vinaigre.
luh vee-NEH-gruh.

402. The mustard.
La moutarde.
la moo-tard.

403. The garlic.
L'ail.
LAH-yuh.

BREAKFAST FOODS

404. May I have some fruit juice?
Puis-je avoir du jus de fruit?
PWEE-zhuh a-vwahr dew zhew duh frwee?

405. —— Some orange juice.
Du jus d'orange.
dew zhew daw-rahnzh.

406. —— Some tomato juice.
Du jus de tomate.
dew zhew duh taw-maht.

407. —— Some stewed prunes.
Des pruneaux cuits.
day prew-noh kwee.

408. —— Some cooked cereal.
Des céréales cuites.
day say-ray-al kweet.

409. —— Some toast and jam.
Du toast avec de la confiture.
dew tohst a-vek duh la kawn-fee-tewr.

410. —— Some rolls.
Des petits pains.
day puh-tee pen.

411. —— An omelet.
Une omelette.
ewn awm-let.

412. —— Some soft-boiled eggs.
Des œufs à la coque.
day zuh ah la kawk.

413. —— Some medium-boiled eggs.
Des œufs quatre minutes.
day zhuh KA-truh mee-newt.

414. —— Some hard-boiled eggs.
Des œufs durs.
day zuh dewr.

415. —— Some fried eggs.
Des œufs sur le plat.
day zuh sewr luh pla.

416. —— Some scrambled eggs.
Des œufs brouillés.
day zuh broo-yay.

417. —— Some bacon and eggs.
Des œufs avec du lard.
day zuh a-vek dew lar.

418. —— **Some ham and eggs.**
Des œufs au jambon.
day zuh oh zhahn-bawn.

SOUPS AND ENTRÉES

419. I want some chicken soup.
Je désire du potage au poulet.
zhuh day-zeer dew paw-tazh oh poo-leh.

420. —— **Some vegetable soup.**
Du potage aux légumes.
dew paw-tazh oh lay-gewm.

421. —— **Some roast chicken.**
Du poulet rôti.
dew poo-leh roh-tee.

422. —— **Some fried chicken.**
Du poulet frit.
dew poo-leh free.

423. —— **Some beef.**
Du bœuf.
dew buhf.

424. —— **Some duck.**
Du canard.
dew ka-nar.

425. —— **Some goose.**
De l'oie.
duh lwah.

426. —— **Some lamb.**
Du gigot.
dew zhee-goh.

427. —— **Some liver.**
Du foie.
dew fwah.

428. —— **Some lobster.**
Du homard.
dew aw-mar.

429. —— **Some pork.**
Du porc.
dew pawr.

430. —— **Some roast beef.**
Du rosbif.
dew raws-beef.

431. —— **Some sardines.**
Des sardines.
day sar-deen.

432. —— **Some sausage.**
De la saucisse.
duh la saw-seess.

433. —— **Some shrimps.**
Des crevettes.
day kruh-vet.

434. —— **Some steak.**
Du bifteck.
dew bif-tek.

435. —— **Some veal.**
Du veau.
dew voh.

VEGETABLES AND SALAD

436. I want some asparagus.
Je désire des asperges.
zhuh day-zeer day zas-pehrzh.

437. —— Some beans.
Des haricots.
day a-ri-koh.

438. —— Some cabbage.
Du chou.
dew shoo.

439. —— Some carrots.
Des carottes.
day ka-rawt.

440. —— Some cauliflower.
Du chou-fleur.
dew shoo-fluhr.

441. —— Some celery and olives.
Du céleri et des olives.
dew sayl-ree ay day zaw-leev.

442. —— Some cucumber.
Du concombre.
dew kawn-KAWN-bruh.

443. —— Some lettuce.
De la laitue.
duh la leh-tew.

444. —— Some mushrooms.
Des champignons.
day shahn-peen-yawn.

445. —— Some onions.
Des oignons.
day zawn-yawn.

446. —— Some peas.
Des petits pois.
day puh-tee pwah.

447. —— Some peppers.
Des poivrons.
day pwahv-rawn.

448. —— Some boiled potatoes.
Des pommes de terre bouillies.
day pawm duh tehr boo-yee.

449. —— Some fried potatoes.
Des pommes de terre frites.
day pawm duh tehr freet.

450. —— Some mashed potatoes.
De la purée de pommes de terre.
duh la pew-ray duh pawm duh tehr.

451. —— Some rice.
Du riz.
dew ree.

452. —— Some spinach.
Des épinards.
day zay-pee-nahr.

453. —— **Some tomatos.**
Des tomates.
day taw-maht.

FRUITS

454. I want an apple.
Je désire une pomme.
zhuh day-zee rewn pawm.

455. —— **Some cherries.**
Des cerises.
day suh-reez.

456. —— **A grapefruit.**
Une pamplemousse.
ewn pahn-pluh-mooss.

457. —— **Some grapes.**
Du raisin.
dew ray-zen.

458. —— **Some lemon.**
Du citron.
dew see-trawn.

459. —— **Some melon.**
Du melon.
dew muh-lawn.

460. —— **Some nuts (walnuts).**
Des noix.
day nwah.

461. —— **An orange.**
Une orange.
ew naw-rahnzh.

462. —— **A peach.**
Une pêche.
ewn pesh.

463. —— **Some raspberries.**
Des framboises.
day frahn-bwahz.

464. —— **Some strawberries.**
Des fraises.
day frez.

BEVERAGES

465. —— **Some black coffee.**
Du café noir.
dew ka-fay nwahr.

466. —— **Coffee with cream.**
Un café crème.
uhn ka-fay krem.

467. —— **Some milk.**
Du lait.
dew leh.

468. —— **Some tea.**
Du thé.
dew tay.

469. —— **Some lemonade**
De la citronnade.
duh la see-traw-nad.

DESSERTS

470. May I have some cake?
Puis-je avoir du gâteau?
PWEE-zhah-vwahr dew gah-toh?

471. —— **Some cheese.**
Du fromage.
dew fraw-mazh.

472. —— **Some cookies.**
De petits gâteaux secs.
duh puh-tee gah-toh sek.

473. —— **Some crepes suzette.**
Des crêpes Suzette.
day krep sew-zet.

474. —— **Some custard.**
De la crème renversée.
duh la krem rahn-vehr-say.

475. —— **Some chocolate ice cream.**
De la glace au chocolat.
duh la glas oh shaw-kaw-la.

476. —— **Some vanilla ice cream.**
De la glace à la vanille.
duh la glas ah la va-NEE-yuh.

CHURCH

477. I would like to go to church.
Je voudrais aller à l'église.
zhuh voo-dreh zal-lay ah lay-gleez.

478. A Catholic church.
Une église catholique.
ewn ay-gleez ka-taw-leek.

479. A Protestant (Anglican) church.
Un temple protestant (anglican).
uhn TAHN-pluh praw-tes-tahn (ahn-glee-kahn).

480. A synagogue.
Une synagogue.
ewn see-na-gawg.

481. When is the service (mass)?
Quelle est l'heure de l'office (de la messe)?
keh leh luhr duh law-feess (duh la mess)?

482. Is there an English-speaking priest (rabbi, minister)?
Y a-t-il un prêtre (un rabbin, un pasteur) qui parle anglais?
ee a-tee luhn PREH-truh (uhn ra-ben, uhn pas-tuhr) kee par lahn-gleh?

SIGHTSEEING

483. I want a guide who speaks English.
Je désire un guide qui parle anglais.
zhuh day-zeer uhn gheed kee par lahn-gleh.

484. What is the charge per hour (day)?
Quel est le prix de l'heure (de la journée)?
keh leh luh pree duh luhr (duh la zhoor-nay)?

485. I am interested in painting.
Je m'intéresse à la peinture.
zhuh men-tay-ress ah la pen-tewr.

486. —— Sculpture.
La sculpture.
la skewl-tewr.

487. —— Architecture.
L'architecture.
lar-shee-tek-tewr.

488. —— The castle.
Le château.
luh shah-toh.

489. —— The cathedral.
La cathédrale.
la ka-tay-dral.

490. —— The museum.
Le musée.
luh mew-zay.

491. When does it open, close?
À quelle heure est l'ouverture, la fermeture?
a keh luhr eh loo-vehr-tewr, la fehrm-tewr?

492. Where is the entrance, exit?
Où est l'entrée, la sortie?
oo eh lahn-tray, la sawr-tee?

493. What is the price of admission?
Quel est le prix d'entrée?
keh leh luh pree dahn-tray?

AMUSEMENTS

494. I should like to go to a concert.
Je voudrais aller à un concert.
zhuh voo-dreh zal-lay ah uhn kawn-sehr.

495. —— To the movies.
Au cinéma.
oh see-nay-ma.

496. —— To a night club.
Dans une boîte de nuit.
dahn zewn bwaht duh nwee.

497. —— To the opera.
À l'opéra.
ah loh-pay-ra.

498. —— To the theater.
Au théâtre.
oh tay-AH-truh.

499. At the box office.
Au bureau de location.
oh bew-roh duh law-ka-syawn.

500. Is there a matinee today?
Y a-t-il matinée aujourd'hui?
ee a-teel ma-tee-nay oh-zhourd-wee?

501. When does the evening performance, the floor show start?
À quelle heure commence la soirée, le spectacle?
ah keh luhr kaw-mahns la swah-ray, luh spek-TA-kluh?

502. Have you any seats for tonight?
Avez-vous des places pour ce soir?
ah-vay-voo day plass poor suh swahr?

503. An orchestra seat.
Un fauteuil d'orchestre.
uhn foh-TUH-yuh dawr-KES-truh.

504. A reserved seat.
Une place réservée.
ewn plas ray-zehr-vay.

505. In the balcony.
Au balcon.
oh bal-kawn.

506. The box.
La loge.
la lawzh.

507. Can I see well from there?
Pourrai-je bien voir de cet endroit?
poo-RAY-zhuh byen vwahr duh set ahn-drwah?

508. Where can we go to dance?
Où pouvons-nous aller danser?
oo poo-vawn-noo al-lay dahn-say?

509. May I have this dance?
Voulez-vous danser?
voo-lay-voo dahn-say?

SPORTS

510. The beach.
La plage.
la plazh.

511. Fishing.
La pêche.
la pesh.

512. Golf.
Le golf.
luh gawlf.

513. Horse racing.
Les courses.
lay koorss.

514. Skating.
Le patinage.
luh pa-tee-nazh.

515. Skiing.
Le ski.
luh skee.

516. Soccer.
Le football.
luh foot-bal.

517. Swimming.
La natation.
la na-ta-syawn.

518. Swimming pool.
La piscine.
la pee-seen.

519. Tennis.
Le tennis.
luh teh-neess.

BANK AND MONEY

520. Where is the nearest bank?
Où est la banque la plus proche?
oo eh la bahnk la plew prawsh?

521. At which window can I cash this?
À quel guichet puis-je toucher ceci?
ah kel ghee-sheh PWEE-zhuh too-shay suh-see?

522. Can you change this for me?
Pouvez-vous me changer ceci?
poo-vay-voo muh shahn-zhay suh-see?

523. Will you cash a check?
Voulez-vous payer un chèque?
voo-lay-voo pay-yay uhn shek?

524. Do not give me large bills.
Ne me donnez pas de gros billets.
nuh muh daw-nay pah duh groh bee-yeh.

525. May I have some change?
Puis-je avoir de la petite monnaie?
pwee-zha-vwahr duh la puh-teet maw-neh?

526. I have traveler's checks.
J'ai des chèques de voyageur.
zhay day shek duh vwah-ya-zhuhr.

527. A letter of credit.
Une lettre de crédit.
ewn LEH-truh duh kray-dee.

528. A bank draft.
Une lettre de change.
ewn LEH-truh duh shahnzh.

529. What is the exchange rate on the dollar?
Quel est le cours du change?
keh leh luh koor dew shahnzh?

530. May I have twenty dollars' worth of French money?
Puis-je avoir vingt dollars en argent français?
pwee-zhah-vwahr ven daw-lahr ah nar-zhant frahn-seh?

USEFUL SHOPPING INFORMATION

531. I want to go shopping.
Je veux courir les magasins.
zhuh vuh koo-reer lay ma-ga-zen.

532. I like that.
J'aime cela.
zhem suh-la.

533. How much is it?
Combien est-ce?
kawn-byen ess?

534. It is very expensive.
C'est très cher.
seh treh shehr.

535. I prefer something better (cheaper).
Je préfère quelque chose de mieux (de moins cher).
zhuh pray-fehr kel-kuh-shohz duh myuh (duh mwen shehr).

536. Show me some others.
Montrez-m'en d'autres.
mawn-tray-mahn DOH-truh.

537. May I try this on?
Puis-je l'essayer?
PWEE-zhuh leh-say-yay?

538. Can I order one?
Puis-je en commander un?
pwee-zhahn kaw-mahn-day uhn?

539. How long will it take?
Combien de temps cela prendra-t-il?
kawn-byen duh tahn suh-la prahn-drah-teel?

540. Please take my measurements.
Veuillez prendre mes mesures.
vuh-yay PRĀHN-druh may muh-zewr.

541. Can you ship it to New York City?
Pouvez-vous l'expédier à New-York ?
poo-vay-voo lex-pay-dyay ah New York?

542. Whom do I pay?
À qui dois-je payer ?
ah kee DWAH-zhuh peh-yay?

543. Please bill me.
Veuillez m'envoyer la facture.
vuh-yay mahn-vwah-yay la fak-tewr.

544. I want to buy a bathing cap.
Je veux acheter un bonnet de bain.
zhuh vuh zash-tay uhn baw-neh duh ben.

545. —— A bathing suit.
Un costume de bain.
uhn kawss-tewm duh ben.

546. —— A blouse.
Une blouse.
ewn blooz.

547. —— A brassiere.
Un soutien-gorge.
uhn soo-tyen-gawrzh.

548. —— A coat.
Un manteau.
uhn mahn-toh.

549. —— A dress.
Une robe.
ewn rawb.

550. —— A pair of gloves.
Une paire de gants.
ewn pehr duh gahn.

551. —— A handbag.
Un sac à main.
uhn sak ah men.

552. —— Some handkerchiefs.
Des mouchoirs.
day moo-shwahr.

553. —— A hat.
Un chapeau.
uhn sha-poh.

554. —— A jacket.
Une jaquette.
ewn zha-ket.

555. —— Some lingerie.
De la lingerie.
duh la lenzh-ree.

556. —— A nightgown.
Une chemise de nuit.
ewn shuh-meez duh nwee.

557. —— A raincoat.
Un imperméable.
uh nen-pehr-may-AH-bluh.

558. —— A pair of shoes.
Une paire de chaussures.
ewn pehr duh shoh-sewr.

559. —— **Some shoelaces.**
Des lacets.
day la-seh.

560. —— **A pair of slippers.**
Une paire de pantoufles.
ewn pehr duh pahn-TOO-fluh.

561. —— **A pair of socks.**
Une paire de chaussettes.
ewn pehr duh shoh-set.

562. —— **A pair of nylon stockings.**
Une paire de bas nylon.
ewn pehr duh bah nee-lawn.

563. —— **A suit.**
Un costume.
uhn kawss-tewm.

564. —— **A sweater.**
Un sweater.
uhn sweh-tuhr.

565. —— **Some ties.**
Des cravates.
day krah-vaht.

566. —— **Trousers.**
Un pantalon.
uhn pahn-ta-lawn.

567. —— **Some underwear.**
Des sous-vêtements.
day soo-vet-mahn.

568. Do you have some ashtrays?
Avez-vous des cendriers?
a-vay-voo day sahn-dree-ay?

569. —— **A box of candy.**
Une boîte de bonbons.
ewn bwaht duh bawn-bawn.

570. —— **Some china.**
De la porcelaine.
duh la pawr-suh-len.

571. —— **Some dolls.**
Des poupées.
day poo-pay.

572. —— **Some earrings.**
Des boucles d'oreille.
day BOO-kluh daw-ray.

573. —— **Some perfume.**
Du parfum.
dew par-fuhn.

574. —— **Some pictures.**
Des tableaux.
day ta-bloh.

575. —— **Some records.**
Des disques.
day deesk.

576. —— **Some silverware.**
De l'argenterie.
duh lar-zhahn-tree.

577. —— **Some toys.**
Des jouets.
day zhoo-eh.

578. —— **An umbrella.**
Un parapluie.
uhn pa-ra-plwee.

579. —— **A watch.**
Une montre.
ewn MAWN-truh.

MEASUREMENTS

580. What is the length?
Quelle est la longueur?
keh leh la lawn-guhr?

581. —— The width?
La largeur?
la lar-zhuhr?

582. —— The size?
La pointure?
la pwen-tewr?

583. How much is it per meter?
Combien le mètre?
kawn-byen luh MEH-truh?

584. It is ten meters long by four meters wide.
Il a dix mètres de long sur quatre mètres de large.
eel a dee MEH-truh duh lawn sewr KA-truh MEH-truh duh larzh.

585. High.
Haut.
oh.

586. Low.
Bas.
bah.

587. Large.
Grand.
grahn.

588. Small.
Petit.
puh-tee.

589. Medium.
Moyen.
mwah-yen.

590. Alike.
Semblable.
sahn-BLA-bluh.

591. Different.
Différent.
dee-fay-rahn.

592. A pair.
Une paire.
ewn pehr.

593. A dozen.
Une douzaine.
ewn doo-zen.

594. Half a dozen.
Une demi-douzaine.
ewn duh-mee-doo-zen.

COLORS

595. I want a lighter shade.
Je désire un ton plus clair.
zhuh day-zeer uhn tawn plew klehr.

596. —— A darker shade.
Un ton plus foncé.
uhn tawn plew fawn-say.

597. Black.
Noir.
nwahr.

598. Blue.
Bleu.
bluh.

599. Brown.
Brun.
bruhn.

600. Gray.
Gris.
gree.

601. Green.
Vert.
vehr.

602. Orange.
Orange.
aw-rahnzh.

603. Pink.
Rose.
rohz.

604. Purple.
Violet.
vyaw-leh.

605. Red.
Rouge.
roozh.

606. White.
Blanc.
blahn.

607. Yellow.
Jaune.
zhohn.

STORES

608. Where is the bakery?
Où est la boulangerie?
oo eh la boo-lahnzh-ree?

609. —— The pastry shop.
La pâtisserie.
la pah-teess-ree.

610. —— A candy store.
Une confiserie.
ewn kawn-feez-ree.

611. —— A cigar store.
Un bureau de tabac.
uhn bew-roh duh ta-bah.

612. —— A clothing store.
Un magasin d'habillement.
uhn ma-ga-zen dah-bee-yuh-mahn.

613. —— A department store.
Un grand magasin.
uhn grahn ma-ga-zen.

614. —— A drugstore.
Une pharmacie.
ewn far-ma-see.

615. —— A grocery.
Une épicerie.
ewn ay-peess-ree.

616. —— A hardware store.
Une quincaillerie.
ewn ken-kah-yuh-ree.

617. —— A hat shop.
Une chapellerie.
ewn sha-pel-ree.

618. —— A jewelry store.
Une bijouterie.
ewn bee-zhoo-tree.

619. —— A meat market.
Une boucherie.
ewn boosh-ree.

620. —— A shoemaker.
Un cordonnier.
uhn kawr-daw-nyay.

621. —— **A shoe store.**
Un magasin de chaussures.
uhn ma-ga-zen duh shoh-sewr.

622. —— **A tailor shop.**
Un tailleur.
uhn ta-yuhr.

623. —— **A watchmaker.**
Un horloger.
uh nawr-law-zhay.

BOOKSTORE AND STATIONER'S

624. Where is there a bookstore?
Où se trouve une librairie?
oo suh troov ewn lee-bray-ree?

625. —— **A stationer's.**
Une papeterie.
ewn pap-tree.

626. —— **A news dealer.**
Un marchand de journaux.
uhn mar-shahn duh zhoor-noh.

627. I want to buy a newspaper.
Je désire acheter un journal.
zhuh day-zee rash-tay uhn zhoor-nal.

628. —— **A magazine.**
Une revue.
ewn ruh-vew.

629. —— **A dictionary.**
Un dictionnaire.
uhn deek-syaw-nayr.

630. —— **A guidebook.**
Un guide.
uhn gheed.

631. —— **A book.**
Un livre.
uhn LEE-vruh.

632. —— **A map of Paris.**
Un plan de Paris.
uhn plahn duh pa-ree.

633. I would like some postcards.
Je voudrais des cartes postales.
zhuh voo-dreh day kart paws-tal.

634. —— **Some writing paper.**
Du papier à lettre.
dew pap-yay ah LEH-truh.

635. —— **A pencil.**
Un crayon.
uhn kreh-yawn.

636. —— **A fountain pen.**
Un stylo.
uhn stee-loh.

637. —— **Some envelopes (airmail).**
Des enveloppes (avion).
day zahn-vuh-lawp (a-vyawn).

CIGAR STORE

638. Where is the nearest cigar store?
Où est le bureau de tabac le plus proche?
oo eh luh bew-roh duh ta-bah luh plew prawsh?

639. I want some cigars.
Je veux des cigares.
zhuh vuh day see-gar.

640. —— Some pipe tobacco.
Du tabac pour la pipe.
dew ta-bah poor la peep.

641. —— Some cigarette cases.
Des étuis à cigarettes.
day zay-twee ah see-ga-ret.

642. —— A lighter.
Un briquet.
uhn bree-keh.

643. —— A pack of American cigarettes.
Un paquet de cigarettes américaines.
uhn pa-keh duh see-ga-ret za-may-ree-ken.

644. Do you have a match?
Avez-vous une allumette?
a-vay-voo zewn al-lew-met?

PHOTOGRAPHY

645. I want a roll of (color) film.
Je désire un rouleau de pellicules (en couleurs).
zhuh day-zeer uhn roo-loh duh pel-lee-kewl (ahn koo luhr).

646. Some movie film.
Des pellicules cinékodak.
day pel-lee-kewl see-nay-kaw-dak.

647. For this camera.
Pour cet appareil.
poor seh ta-pa-ray.

648. What is the charge for developing a roll?
Combien prenez-vous pour développer une bobine?
kawn-byen pruh-nay-voo poor dayv-law-pay ewn baw-been?

649. When will they be ready?
Quand seront-ils prêts?
kahn suh-rawn-teel preh?

DRUGSTORE

650. Where is there a drugstore where they understand English?
Où y a-t-il une pharmacie où l'on comprend l'anglais?
oo ee a-tee lewn far-ma-see oo lawn kawn-prahn lahn-gleh?

651. Can you fill this prescription?
Pouvez-vous remplir cette ordonnance?
poo-vay-voo rahn-pleer set awr-daw-nahns?

652. How long will it take?
Combien de temps vous faudra-t-il?
kawn-byen duh tahn voo foh-dra-teel?

653. I want some adhesive tape.
Je veux du sparadrap.
zhuh vuh dew spa-ra-drah.

654. —— Some alcohol.
De l'alcool.
duh lal-kawl.

655. —— An antiseptic.
Un antiseptique.
uh nahn-tee-sep-teek.

656. —— Some aspirin.
De l'aspirine.
duh las-pee-reen.

657. —— Some bobby pins.
Des épingles à cheveux.
day zay-PEN-gluh zah shuh-vuh.

658. —— Some cleaning fluid.
Un produit pour détacher.
uhn praw-dwee poor day-ta-shay.

659. —— Some cold cream.
Du cold-cream.
dew "cold cream."

660. —— A comb.
Un peigne.
uhn PEN-yuh.

661. —— Some corn pads.
Des toiles anticor.
day twahl ahn-tee-kawr.

662. —— Some cotton.
De l'ouate.
duh loo-wat.

663. —— A deodorant.
Un désodorisant.
uhn day-zaw-daw-ree-zahn.

664. —— An ice bag.
Un sac à glace.
uhn sak ah glas.

665. —— **Some iodine.**
De l'iode.
duh lee-awd.

666. —— **A mild laxative.**
Un laxatif doux.
uhn lax-ah-teef doo.

667. —— **Some lipstick.**
Du rouge à lèvres.
dew roozh ah LEH-vruh.

668. —— **Some safety pins.**
Des épingles de sûreté.
day zay-PEN-gluh duh sewr-tay.

669. —— **Some powder.**
Du talc.
dew talk.

670. —— **A razor.**
Un rasoir.
uhn ra-zwahr.

671. —— **Some razor blades.**
Des lames de rasoir.
day lam duh ra-zwahr.

672. —— **Some sanitary napkins.**
Des serviettes hygiéniques.
day sehr-vee-et zee-zhee-ay-neek.

673. —— **A sedative.**
Un calmant.
uhn kal-mahn.

674. —— **A bottle of shampoo.**
Un flacon de shampooing.
uhn fla-kawn duh shahn-pwen.

675. —— **A shaving lotion.**
Une lotion après la barbe.
ewn law-syawn a-preh la barb.

676. —— **Some shaving cream (brushless).**
De la crème à raser (à appliquer sans blaireau).
duh la krem ah rah-zay (ah ap-plee-kay sahn blay-roh).

677. —— **Some sunglasses.**
Des lunettes de soleil.
day lew-net duh saw-lay.

678. —— **Some suntan oil.**
De l'huile de soleil.
duh lweel duh saw-lay.

679. —— **A thermometer.**
Un thermomètre.
uhn tehr-maw-MEH-truh.

680. —— **(A tube of) toothpaste.**
(Un tube de) pâte dentifrice.
(uhn tewb duh) paht dahn-tee-freess.

LAUNDRY AND DRY CLEANING

681. Where is the nearest laundry?
Où est la blanchisserie la plus proche?
oo eh la blahn-sheess-ree la plew prawsh?

682. —— The dry cleaner.
La teinturerie.
la ten-tewr-ree.

683. Could I have some laundry done?
Puis-je faire laver des affaires?
PWEE-zhuh fehr la-vay day za-fehr?

684. To be washed, mended.
À faire laver, repriser.
ah fehr la-vay, ruh-pree-zay.

685. To be cleaned, pressed.
À faire nettoyer, repasser.
ah fehr neh-twah-yay, ruh-pas-say.

686. The belt is missing.
La ceinture manque.
la sen-tewr mahnk.

687. Can you sew on this button?
Pouvez-vous me coudre ce bouton?
poo-vay-voo muh KOO-druh suh boo-tawn?

688. —— The zipper.
La fermeture éclair.
la fehrm-tew ray-klehr.

BARBER SHOP AND BEAUTY PARLOR

689. Where is there a good barber?
Où se trouve un bon coiffeur?
oo suh troov uhn bawn kwah-fuhr?

690. A haircut, please.
Une coupe de cheveux, s'il vous plaît.
ewn koop duh shuh-vuh, seel voo pleh.

691. A shave, please.
Une barbe, s'il vous plaît.
ewn barb, seel voo pleh.

692. A shampoo.
Un shampooing.
uhn shahn-pwen.

693. A permanent.
Une permanente.
ewn pehr-ma-nahnt.

694. A facial.
Un massage facial.
uhn mas-sazh fa-syal.

695. A manicurist, please.
Une manucure, s'il vous plaît.
ewn ma-new-kewr, seel voo pleh.

696. I want a shoe shine.
Je veux faire cirer mes chaussures.
zhuh vuh fehr see-ray may shoh-sewr.

697. May I make an appointment for tomorrow?
Puis-je prendre rendez-vous pour demain?
PWEE-zhuh PRAHN-druh rahn-day-voo poor duh-men?

HEALTH AND ILLNESS

698. I wish to see an American doctor.
Je désire voir un docteur américain.
zhuh day-zeer vwahr uhn dawk-tuh ra-may-ree-ken.

699. I do not sleep well.
Je ne dors pas bien.
zhuh nuh dawr pah byen.

700. My head aches.
J'ai mal à la tête.
zhay mal ah la tet.

701. Must I stay in bed?
Dois-je rester au lit?
DWAH-zhuh res-tay oh lee?

702. May I get up?
Puis-je me lever?
PWEE-zhuh muh luh-vay?

703. I feel better.
Je me sens mieux.
zhuh muh sahn myuh.

DENTIST

704. Do you know a good dentist?
Connaissez-vous un bon dentiste?
kaw-nes-say-voo uhn bawn dahn-teest?

705. This tooth hurts.
Cette dent me fait mal.
set dahn muh feh mal.

706. Can you fix it (temporarily)?
Pouvez-vous l'arranger (provisoirement)?
poo-vay-voo lar-rahn-zhay (praw-vee-zwahr-mahn)?

707. I have lost a filling.
J'ai perdu un plombage.
zhay pehr-dew uhn plawn-bazh.

708. I do not want this tooth extracted.
Je ne veux pas faire arracher cette dent.
zhuh nuh vuh pah feh rar-ra-shay set dahn.

POST OFFICE

709. Where is the post office?
Où est la poste?
oo eh la pawst?

710. A letter to the United States.
Une lettre pour les Etats-Unis.
ewn LEH-truh poor lay zay-tah-zew-nee.

711. How many stamps do I need?
A combien dois-je l'affranchir?
a kawn-byen DWAH-zhuh laf-rahn-sheer?

712. Three stamps of 15 franc denomination.
Trois timbres de quinze francs.
trwah TEN-bruh duh kenz frahn.

713. I want to send a money order.
Je désire envoyer un mandat-poste.
zhuh day-zee rahn-vwah-yay uhn mahn-da-pawst.

714. Give me a receipt, please.
Donnez-moi un récépissé, s'il vous plaît.
daw-nay-mwah uhn ray-say-pees-say, seel voo pleh.

715. By airmail.
Par avion.
pa rah-vyawn.

716. Parcel post.
Par colis postal.
par kaw-lee paws-tal.

TELEPHONE

717. Where can I telephone?
Où puis-je téléphoner?
oo PWEE-zhuh tay-lay-faw-nay?

718. Will you telephone for me?
Voulez-vous bien téléphoner pour moi?
voo-lay-voo byen tay-lay-faw-nay poor mwah?

719. I want to make a local call, number ——.
Donnez-moi la ville, numéro ——.
daw-nay-mwah la veel, new-may-roh ——.

720. May I speak to Leon?
Puis-je parler à Léon?
PWEE-zhuh par-lay ah lay-awn?

TIME AND TIME EXPRESSIONS

721. What time is it?
Quelle heure est-il?
keh luh reh-teel?

722. It is two o'clock A.M., P.M.
Il est deux heures du matin, de l'après-midi.
eel eh duh zuhr dew ma-ten, duh la-preh-mee-dee.

723. It is half past three.
Il est trois heures et demie.
eel eh trwah zuhr ay duh-mee.

724. It is a quarter past four.
Il est quatre heures et quart.
eel eh kat ruhr ay kar.

725. It is a quarter to five.
Il est cinq heures moins le quart.
eel eh sen kuhr mwen luh kar.

726. At ten minutes to six.
À six heures moins dix.
ah see zuhr mwen deess.

727. At ten minutes past seven.
À sept heures dix.
ah seh tuhr deess.

DAYS OF THE WEEK

728. Monday.
Lundi.
luhn-dee.

729. Tuesday.
Mardi.
mar-dee.

730. Wednesday.
Mercredi.
mehr-kruh-dee.

731. Thursday.
Jeudi.
zhuh-dee.

732. Friday.
Vendredi.
vahn-druh-dee.

733. Saturday.
Samedi.
sam-dee.

734. Sunday.
Dimanche.
dee-mahnsh.

MONTHS AND SEASONS

735. January.
Janvier.
zhahn-vee-ay.

736. February.
Février.
fayv-ree-ay.

737. March.
Mars.
marss.

738. April.
Avril.
av-reel.

739. May.
Mai.
may.

740. June.
Juin.
zhwen.

741. July.
Juillet.
zhwee-yeh.

742. August.
Août.
oo.

743. September.
Septembre.
sep-TAHN-bruh.

744. October.
Octobre.
awk-TAW-bruh.

745. November.
Novembre.
naw-VAHN-bruh.

746. December.
Décembre.
day-SAHN-bruh.

747. Spring.
Le printemps.
luh pren-tahn.

748. Summer.
L'été.
lay-tay.

749. Autumn.
L'automne.
law-tawn.

750. Winter.
L'hiver.
lee-vehr.

751. NUMBERS.

One. Un. *uhn.*　　**Two.** Deux. *duh.*　　**Three.** Trois. *trwah.*

Four. Quatre. *KA-truh.*　　**Five.** Cinq. *senk.*

Six. Six. *seess.*　　**Seven.** Sept. *set.*　　**Eight.** Huit. *weet.*

Nine. Neuf. *nuhf.*　　**Ten.** Dix. *deess.*

Eleven. Onze. *awnz.*　　**Twelve.** Douze. *dooz.*

Thirteen. Treize. *trez.*　　**Fourteen.** Quatorze. *ka-tawrz.*

Fifteen. Quinze. *kenz.*　　**Sixteen.** Seize. *sez.*

Seventeen. Dix-sept. *dee-set.*　　**Eighteen.** Dix-huit. *dee-zweet.*

Nineteen. Dix-neuf. *deez-nuhf.*　　**Twenty.** Vingt. *ven.*

Twenty-one. Vingt et un. *ven-tay-uhn.*

Twenty-two. Vingt-deux. *vent-duh.*　　**Thirty.** Trente. *trahnt.*

Thirty-one. Trente et un. *trahn-tay-uhn.*

Forty. Quarante. *ka-rahnt.*　　**Fifty.** Cinquante. *sen-kahnt.*

Sixty. Soixante. *swa-sahnt.*

Seventy. Soixante-dix. *swa-sahnt-deess.*

Seventy-one. Soixante et onze. *swa-sahn tay awnz.*

Eighty. Quatre-vingts. *ka-truh-ven.*

Eighty-one. Quatre-vingt-un. *ka-truh-ven-uhn.*

Ninety. Quatre-vingt-dix. *ka-truh-ven-deess.*

Ninety-one. Quatre-vingt-onze. *ka-truh-ven- awnz.*

Ninety-two. Quatre-vingt-douze. *ka-truh-ven- dooz.*

One hundred. Cent. *sahn.*

Two hundred. Deux cents. *duh sahn.*

One thousand. Mille. *meel.*

Two thousand. Deux mille. *duh meel.*

INDEX

The sentences, words and phrases in this book are numbered consecutively from 1 to 751. All entries in this book refer to these numbers. In addition, each major section heading (CAPITALIZED) is indexed according to page number (**boldface**). Parts of speech are indicated by the following italic abbreviations: *adj.* for adjective, *adv.* for adverb, *n.* for noun and *v.* for verb. Parentheses are used for explanations.

Because of the large volume of material indexed, cross-indexing has generally been avoided. Phrases or groups of words will usually be found under only one of their components, e.g., "bathing suit" appears only under "bathing," even though there is a separate entry for "suit" alone. If you do not find a phrase under one word, try another.

Accept 337
address 37; mailing — 61
adjust 277
admission 493
ahead, straight 200
air-conditioned 293
airline office 173
airmail, by 715
AIRPLANE **p. 23**
airport 175, 232
alcohol 654
alike 590
all 78; — right 29, 73
A.M. 722
am, I 22
American 643
AMUSEMENTS **p. 41**
and 27
Anglican 479
another (additional) 321;
    let's have — 348
antiseptic 655
anyone 41
apartment 288
apple 454
appointment 7
April 738
architecture 487
arrive 179
ashtray 568

ask 383
asparagus 436
aspirin 656
August 742
aunt 35
AUTOMOBILE
    TRAVEL **p. 25**
autumn 749
avenue 207

Back *adv.* 202
bacon 417
bad 122
bag (luggage) 156
baggage 152; — check
    171; — room 169
bakery 608
balcony 505
bank 520; — draft 528
BANK AND MONEY
    p. 42
barber 689
BARBER SHOP AND
    BEAUTY SALON
    p. 52
bartender 340
bath 299; — mat 327
bathing: — cap 544; —
    suit 545
bathtub 328

beans 437
bed, double 298
beef 423; roast — 430
beer 351
behind 103
bellhop 317
belt 686
beside 104
best 121
better 535; — than 120
BEVERAGES **p. 38**
bill (banknote) 524; (=
    check) 336, 387; *v.* 543
black 597
blanket 321
blouse 546
blue 598
board, go on 222
boarding house 287
BOAT **p. 22**
boat 221; — train 247
bobby pin 657
boiled 448
book *n.* 631
bookstore 624
BOOKSTORE AND
    STATIONER'S **p. 48**
bottle 344, 674
box 569; (theater) 506;
    — office 499

boy 17
brassiere 547
bread 394
breakfast 351
BREAKFAST FOODS
    p. 35
bring 321
broken 144
brother 15
brown 599
brushless 676
bus 253; — service 232;
    — station 175; — stop
    254
BUS, STREETCAR AND
    SUBWAY p. 25
business trip 22
busy 69
butter 395
button 687
buy 544

Cabbage 438
cabin 228
CAFÉ, AT THE p. 31
cake 470
call 150
camera 647
can v.: — I 218; — we
    358; — you 79
captain 224
car 262, 276
carefully 242
carrot 439
cash v. 521, 523
castle 488
cathedral 489
Catholic 478
cauliflower 440
celery 441
center 289
cereal 408
chambermaid 316
change n. (= coins) 525;
    (= the rest) 389; v. (=
    convert money) 522;
    (= exchange) 274, 382;
    (= transfer) 259
charge n. 388, 484; v. 241
cheaper 535
check n. (bank) 337; (=
    bill) 384
cheese 471
cherry 455
chicken 421
child 16
china 570

chocolate 475
CHURCH p. 39
church 478
cigar 639
cigarette 643; — case 641
CIGAR STORE p. 49
circle 205
city 184
class 212
clean v. 685
cleaning fluid 658
close v. 250; when does
    it — 491
clothing 161; — store 612
coat 548
coffee 465
cold adj. 380; — cream
    595; I am — 67
COLORS p. 46
comb 660
come 36, 233, 383; —
    back 320; — here 63;
    — in 64
TELEPHONE p. 55
concert 494
consulate 148
cookie 472
corner 198
corn pad 661
cost v. 209
cotton 662
cream 466
crêpes suzette 473
cucumber 442
custard 474
customs 151
CUSTOMS AND BAG-
    GAGE p. 17

Dance v. 508
darker 596
daughter 11
day 304; per — 484
DAYS OF THE WEEK
    p. 56
December 746
deck 227
declare (customs) 157
DENTIST p. 54
dentist 704
department store 613
DESSERTS p. 39
develop 648
dictionary 629
DIFFICULTIES p. 16
dine 365

diner (= dining car) 251
dinner 353
direct adj. 180
direction 203
do 143
dock 176
doctor 698
doll 571
downstairs 311
dozen 593; half a — 594
draw 271
dress 549
drink n. 341
drive 242
driver 255
driver's license 263
DRUGSTORE p. 50
drugstore 650
dry cleaner 682
duck 424
dutiable 163

Early 130
earrings 572
east 190
egg 412–418
eight 751
eighteen 751
eighty 751
eighty-one 751
elevator 312
eleven 751
empty 107
English (language) 40
English-speaking 482
enjoy 35
entrance 492
envelope 637
everything 159
excellent 390
excess 237
excuse me 57
exit 492
expensive 534
express (train) 216
extract v. 708

Facial n. 694
family 31
far 101; how — 91
faster 134
February 736
feel 703
few 112
fifteen 751
fifty 751
fill (prescription) 651

filling (dental) 707
film 646; color — 645; movie — 646
find 138
finished 166
fine 27
first 212
fishing *n.* 511
five 751
fix 279, 706
floor show 501
food 390
for 718
forget 141
fork 370
forty 751
forward *adv.* 201; *v.* 338
four 751
fourteen 751
French (language) 51; (nationality) 530
Friday 732
fried 422, 449
friend 13, 139
from 95
front: in — of 102
fruit: — drink 342; — juice 404
FRUITS **p.** 38
full 108
furnished 288

Garage 266
garlic 403
gas 272; — station 265
get: — off 260; — up 702
gift 162
girl 18
give 37
glad 21; I am — 70
glass 345
glasses 144
gloves 550
go 173, 268; (= pass) 258
golf 512
good 119, 267
goodbye 4
goose 425
grape 457
grapefruit 456
gray 600
green 601
GREETINGS, INTRODUCTIONS AND SOCIAL CONVERSATION **p.** 10

grocery 615
guide 483
guidebook 630

Haircut 690
half past 723
ham 418
handbag 551
handkerchief 552
hanger 324
hard-boiled 414
hardware store 616
hat 553; — shop 617
have 165, 530, 644
head 700
headwaiter 361
health: — certificate 155; to your — 349
HEALTH AND ILLNESS **p.** 53
hearing aid 146
hello 3
help 79
here 92
high 585
horse racing 513
hotel 83
HOTEL, AT THE **p.** 27
hour, per 241
how 89; — are you 26; — are things 28; — do you say 51; — far 91; — long (time) 90; — much 77
hundred: one — 751; two — 751
hungry, I am 68
hurry, in a 66
hurt 705
husband 10

I 22
ice 392; — bag 664; — cream 475
identification papers 154
immediately 125
in 98
included 385
inexpensive 286
inside 105
interested 485
international 263
introduce 8
iodine 665
it is 73

Jacket 554

jam 409
January 735
jewelry store 618
juice 404–406
July 741
June 740

Keep 389
key 141; room — 332
kilo(gram) 236, 237
kilometer, per 241
knife 371
know (a fact) 74; (be acquainted with) 704; (= make acquaintance with) 21

Ladies' room 82
lamb 426
land *v.* 223
large 587
late 129
later 127
laundry 681; have — done 683
LAUNDRY AND DRY CLEANING **p.** 52
laxative 666
leak *n.* 281
leave 248, 335; (something) 140, 172
left 192
lemon 458
lemonade 469
length 580
less 114
letter 333, 710; — of credit 527
lettuce 443
lifeboat 229
life preserver 230
light *adj.* 346, 595
lighter *n.* 642
like: I — that 532; I — you 39
lingerie 555
lipstick 667
listen 136
liter 272
little, a 115
liver 427
lobster 428
local (train) 215
long 584
look: — for 83; — here 137; — out 135
lose 139

lost-and-found desk 147
lotion 675
low 586
lubricate 276
lunch 352

Magazine 628
make out 336
MAKING YOURSELF
  UNDERSTOOD p. 12
man 19
manager 331
manicurist 695
many 118
map 271
March 737
mass 481
match n. 644
matinée 500
matter: it doesn't — 76;
  what is the — 72
May 739
may I 38
meal 296
mean v. 49
MEASUREMENTS p. 46
measurements, take 540
meat 377; — market 652
mechanic 264
medium (meat) 589
melon 459
mend 684
men's room 81
MENU p. 34
menu 368
message 333
meter, per 583
middle 199
milk 467
mine, be (= belong to
  me) 156
minister 482
miss v. 142
missing, be 686
mistake 387
moment 65
Monday 728
money 141; — order 713
MONTHS AND SEA-
  SONS p. 56
more 113
morning, good 1
movies 495
much: too — 117; very
  — 58
museum 490
mushroom 444

mustard 402
must I 159

Name: my — is 6
near 100
nearest 520
news dealer 626
newspaper 627
next 261, 270
night club 496
nightgown 556
nine 751
nineteen 751
nineteen fifty-six 751
ninety 751
ninety-one 751
no 54
noisy (= noise) 290
north 187
not 45
nothing 110
November 745
now 124
number 334
NUMBERS p. 57
nylon 562

O'clock 318
October 744
oil (food) 400; (lubricat-
  ing) 274
olive 441
omelet 411
on 99
one 751
onion 445
open v. 159; when does
  it — 491
opera 497
orange (color) 602; (fruit)
  461
order v. 381, 538
others 536
outside 106
overheat 282

Pack n. 643
painting 485
pair 592
paper 154; toilet — 330;
  writing — 634
parcel post 716
park v. 284
passport 153
pastry shop 609
pay v. 164
pea 446

peach 462
pen, fountain 636
pencil 635
pepper (seasoning) 398;
  (vegetable) 447
per 237
performance, evening
  501
perfume 573
perhaps 55
permanent n. 693
person 305
PHOTOGRAPHY p. 49
picture 574
piece 152
pillow 322
pillowcase 323
pink 603
pipe 640
place 206
plate 372
please 56
P.M. 722
policeman 150
police station 149
pork 429
port (wine) 345
porter 315
possible, as soon as 128
postcard 633
POST OFFICE p. 54
potato 448–450
powder 669
prefer 535
prescription 651
press v. 685
price 493
priest 482
Protestant 479
prune 407
puncture n. 280
purple 604
purse 140
purser 225

Quarter: — past 724; —
  to 725
quickly 133

Rabbi 482
railroad station 177
raincoat 557
rare (meat) 377
raspberry 463
rate 306; exchange —
  529
razor 670; — blades 671

ready 649
receipt 714
recommend 264
record (phonograph) 575
red 605
regards 35
rent 262
repair 145
repeat 47
reservation 291
reserved 217
restaurant 350
RESTAURANT, AT THE p. 32
rice 451
right (direction) 191
roast *adj.* 421
roll (bread) 410; (film) 645, 648
room 292; double — 295; — number 334; — service 314; single — 294

Safety pin 668
salad 382
salt 397
sandwich 355
sanitary napkin 672
sardine 431
Saturday 733
sauce 399
sausage 432
scrambled 416
sculpture 486
seasick, I am 231
seat 217
second 213
section: business — 181; residential — 182; shopping — 183
see 36
seeing: I'll be — you 5
send 315, 713; — for 313
September 743
serve 357
service 390; (religious) 481; — charge 386
seven 751
· seventeen 751
seventy 751
seventy-one 751
several 111
sew on 687
shade (color) 595
shampoo 674
shave 691

shaving: — cream 676; — lotion 675
ship *v.* 541
shoe 558; — store 621
shoelace 559
shoemaker 620
shoeshine 696
shopping, go 531
show *v.* 181
shower 300
shrimp 433
side 195
SIGHTSEEING p. 40
silverware 576
simple 375
sink *n.* 329
sister 14
sit down 33
six 751
sixteen 751
sixty 751
size 582
skating 514
skiing 515
sleep 699
slipper 560
slowly, more 44
small 588
smoke *v.* 252
snack 356
so, so 30
soap 325
soccer 516
socks 561
soft-boiled 412
soft drink 343
something 109
son 12
soon 126; as — as 128
sorry, I am 71
soup: chicken — 419; vegetable — 420
SOUPS AND ENTRÉES p. 36
south 188
speak 40, 42, 331
spell 52
spicy 376
spinach 452
spoon, large 374
SPORTS p. 42
spring (season) 650
stamp 712
stationer 625
stay 701
steak 434
steward 226

stewed 407
stocking 562
stop *v.* 219, 243
store *v.* 339
STORES p. 47
strawberry 464
street 195; across the — 197
subway 257
sugar 396
suit 563
suite 302
summer 748
Sunday 734
sunglasses 677
suntan oil 678
supper 354
sweater 564
swimming 517; — pool 518
synagogue 480

Table 364; — d'hôte 366
tailor shop 622
take 236, 253; (time) 178, 539; — away 379
tape, adhesive 653
TAXI p. 23
taxi 238
tea 468
teaspoon 374
telephone *v.* 717; — number 37
tell 79
temporarily 706
ten 751
thanks 58
theater 498
there 93; from — 507; — is 161
thermometer 679
these 162
think so 75
third 214
thirsty, I am 68
thirteen 751
thirty 751
thirty-one 751
this 158, 165; — one 309
thousand 751
three 751
Thursday 731
ticket 209; — office 208; one-way — 210; round-trip — 211
TICKETS p. 21
tie *n.* 565

TIME AND TIME EX-
PRESSIONS **p.** 55
time: at what — 233; what
— is it 721
tip *n.* 385
tire *n.* 278; flat — 279
tired, I am 69
to 94
toast 409
tobacco, pipe 640
today 291
tomato 453
tomorrow 339
tonight 303, 502
too (overly) 377
tooth 705
toothpaste 680
towel 326
town 269
toy 577
traffic light 193
TRAIN **p.** 24
train 142
transfer *n.* 256
traveler's check 526
TRAVEL: GENERAL
EXPRESSIONS **p.** 19
traveling 24
trousers 566
try on 537
Tuesday 729
turn 186
twelve 751
twenty 751
twenty-one 751
twenty-two 751

two 751

Umbrella 578
uncle 35
understand 45
underwear 567
U.S.A. 710
until 339
upstairs 310
USEFUL SHOPPING
INFORMATION
p. 43

Vacancy 292
vacation 23
vanilla 476
veal 435
vegetable 420
VEGETABLES AND
SALAD **p.** 37
very 32
village 185
vinegar 401

Wait 65
waiter 360
waitress 359
walk 84
wallet 140
want 172, 365
warm, I am 67
wash 684
washroom 80
watch *n.* 579
watchmaker 623
water 275; mineral — 344

way 180, 181; by — of
218; on the — 219
Wednesday 730
welcome, you are 59
well *adj.* 32; *adv.* 699; —
done (meat) 378
west 189
what 88; — do you wish
62; — is that 50
when 86
where 151
while, for a 284
white 606
who 87
why 85
wide 584
width 581
wife 9
window 249, 521
wine 347; — list 369
winter 750
wish 7, 62
with 96
without 87
woman 20
worse 123
write 48

Yellow 607
yes 53
you 27
your 31

Zipper 688